STAR WARS®

CLONE WARS

VOLUME 8

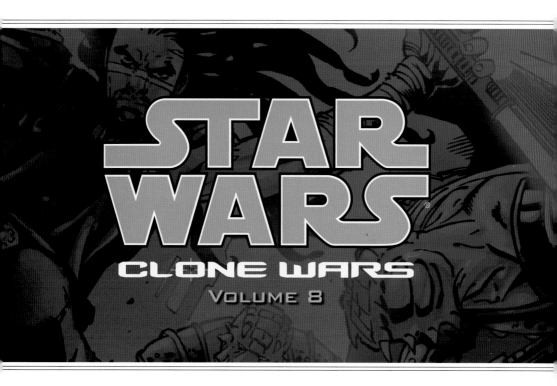

STAR WARS

CLONE WARS
VOLUME 8

The Last Siege, the Final Truth

Dark Horse Books™

colors by **Brad Anderson**

lettering by **Michael David Thomas**

cover illustration by **Tomás Giorello**

publisher **Mike Richardson**

collection designer **Darin Fabrick**

assistant editor **Dave Marshall**

associate editor **Jeremy Barlow**

editor **Randy Stradley**

special thanks to **Sue Rostoni**, **Leland Chee**, and **Amy Gary** at Lucas Licensing

STAR WARS: CLONE WARS VOLUME 8

THIS VOLUME COLLECTS ISSUES #71 THROUGH #77 OF THE DARK HORSE COMIC-BOOK SERIES
STAR WARS: REPUBLIC.

PUBLISHED BY DARK HORSE BOOKS, A DIVISION OF DARK HORSE COMICS, INC.
10956 SE MAIN STREET • MILWAUKIE, OR 97222

WWW.DARKHORSE.COM   WWW.STARWARS.COM
To find a comics shop in your area, call the Comic Shop Locator Service
toll-free at 1-888-266-4226

FIRST EDITION: MARCH 2006 ISBN: 1-59307-482-4

3 5 7 9 10 8 6 4
PRINTED IN CHINA

illustration by **DAVID MICHAEL BECK** and **BRAD ANDERSON**

TRACKDOWN

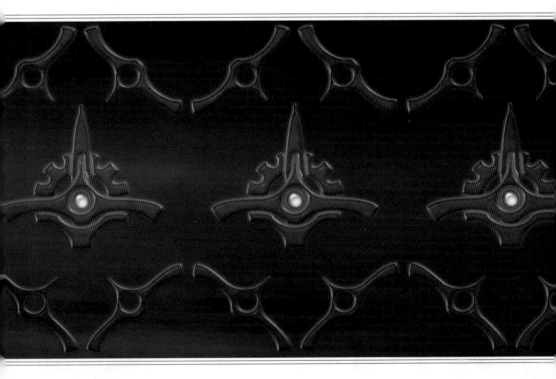

script by **John Ostrander**
pencils by **Jan Duursema**
inks by **Dan Parsons**

THOLME. I NEED YOU PRESENT, THOLME. DO YOU KNOW WHERE YOU ARE?

YES.

YES. I'M ON *NEW HOLSTICE* WITH YOU, *T'RA*, AND MASTER *LUMINARA*. GETTING MY LEG TO WORK AGAIN.

THE CYBERNETIC GRAFTS ARE RESPONDING VERY WELL.

GOOD. I WONDER WHY I DIDN'T DO THIS LONG AGO.

BECAUSE EVERY TIME I BROUGHT IT UP, YOU TOLD ME THAT YOU PREFERRED TO LIMP THAN TO BE MADE INTO SOMETHING YOU ARE NOT.

IS *ANZAT* THAT IMPORTANT?

QUINLAN BROUGHT BACK INFORMATION THAT SORA BULQ HAS MADE SEVERAL TRIPS THERE. THE SEPARATISTS ARE UP TO SOMETHING OUT ON THE RIM -- AND THIS MAY LEAD US TO IT.

I NEED FULL USE OF MY LIMBS IF I'M GOING TO INFILTRATE THE ANZATI.

AND YOU'VE DECIDED THIS IS SOMETHING *YOU* MUST DO BY YOURSELF. UP UNTIL NOW YOU HAVE USED AGENTS...

YES. I'VE KEPT MY HANDS CLEAN. *TOO* CLEAN...

MAGGOT'S CANTINA, ANZAT SPACEPORT...

MY ROUND, BOYS. LISTEN -- I GOT THIS PROBLEM.

I'M SUPPOSED T'MEET UP WITH THIS SEP WEEQUAY, RIGHT? SO I COME ALL TH' WAY HERE -- AND WHERE IS HE? DUNNO. CAN'T FIND HIM. AND YOU ASK ME -- SNOOPING OUTSIDE THE SPACEPORT'S NOT HEALTHY.

NOOO. NOPE. NOT HEALTHY. ANZATI DISCOURAGE IT.

AND THEM WHAT DOES ANYWAY? THEY DON'T USUALLY COME BACK! GET ALL THEIR BRAINS SUCKED OUT, I HEAR!

I KNOW HIM. I SEEN HIM. SHIP'S DOCKED OVER AT A PRIVATE LANDING PAD. UH, HUH!

BUT THIS GUY, HE DON'T FOOL AROUND! DON'T TALK TO NOBODY BUT ANZATI!

NICE LI'L TWI'LEK GIRLIE LIKE JAYZAA DON'T WANT TO MESS AROUND WITH A GUY LIKE THAT! SO I'M NOT GONNA TELL YOU WHERE HE'S AT! SO THERE!

JAYZAA STAY HERE WITH GORT! YAH!

BUT, GORT... SWEETIE. IT WOULD REALLY BE A BIG HELP IF YOU TOLD ME WHERE TO FIND THIS GUY!

AND I'D BE SO GRATEFUL!

IF THEIR MINDS ARE OPENED, IF THEY ARE FOCUSED, WE MAY BE ABLE TO DO MUCH. BUT IT USUALLY TAKES MORE TIME THAN YOU WOULD GIVE US, SORA BULQ.

THE TIME WE HAVE IS WHAT IS GIVEN, *RATH KELKKO* --

WAIT.

WHAT IS IT?

FOR A MOMENT I SENSED... SOMETHING. IT'S GONE NOW.

AND THE MORGUKAI I LEFT GUARDING THE SHIP DOES NOT RESPOND.

PERHAPS HE WANDERED AWAY FROM THE SPACEPORT. IT IS DANGEROUS FOR A NON-ANZATI TO DO SO, BUT IT HAPPENS.

IT'S HIGHLY *UNLIKELY* IN THIS CASE...

...BUT WE CANNOT WAIT. AS I'VE SAID, WE'RE ON A VERY UNFORGIVING TIMETABLE.

THE REPUBLIC'S CLONES HAVE GIVEN THEM THE ADVANTAGE IN THIS WAR.

MY WORK WILL GIVE THE EDGE BACK TO THE SEPARATISTS. BUT IT MUST HAPPEN *SOON* TO BE OF ANY ADVANTAGE.

IF YOU WILL FOLLOW ME...

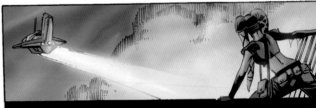

WHAT ARE YOU DOING WITH THE ANZATI, SORA BULQ?

"MASTER THOLME WILL WANT TO KNOW ABOUT THIS."

YOU CHOSE NOT TO KILL THEM.

I KNEW THEY WERE STUDENTS. THEY WERE *EXECUTING* THE FORMS, BUT THEY HAD NOT *MASTERED* THEM. ARE THEY *ALL* YOUR STUDENTS, AKKU SEII?

YES. ALL.

STRANGE. THE TRADITION WAS ALWAYS ONE TEACHER, ONE STUDENT. LIKE A JEDI MASTER AND PADAWAN.

AT THE MOMENT, NO OTHER TEACHERS ARE AVAILABLE.

INDEED?

IT'S BEST YOU LEAVE NOW, THOLME. I AM SORRY I COULD NOT HELP YOU.

YOU HAVE DONE WHAT YOU *COULD* WITHIN THE TRADITIONS, TEACHER. MY THANKS.

LATER...

ANY LUCK WITH THE SHIP'S LOGS I STOLE, MASTER?

MORE PUZZLES THAN ANSWERS, AAYLA. I WAS CERTAIN HE AND HIS FATHER WERE THE *LAST* OF THAT WARRIOR RACE. YOU SAY THE MORGUKAI YOU FOUGHT WAS *NOT* BOK?

I TOOK BOK'S HAND IN BATTLE, MASTER. THIS MORGUKAI *LOOKED* LIKE BOK, BUT HE HAD BOTH HANDS.

YET HE FOUGHT LIKE BOK, AND IN THE MORGUKAI STYLE. HIS WEAPON STOOD UP TO MY SABER LIKE CORTOSIS ALLOY.

AKKU SEII REVEALED AS MUCH AS HE COULD. THERE'S A SHORTAGE OF *TEACHERS* ON ANZAT.

IF SORA BULQ HAS FOUND MORE MORGUKAI AN IS HAVING THE ANZATI TEACH THEM THEIR ASSASSIN TECHNIQUES, THIS COULD BE VERY DANGEROUS.

MY ANALYSIS OF MASTER BULQ'S SHIPS LOG SHOWS HIM VISITING ONE PLANET MORE OFTEN THAN ANY OTHER -- *SALEUCAMI.* IT'S REASONABLE TO ASSUME THAT'S HIS *BASE.*

IT'S *IMPERATIVE* WE LEARN WHAT HE IS DOING THERE.

I HAVE BEEN ORDERE[D] TO *TRIGALIS,* MASTER THOLME.

YOU WOULD BE GOING TO SALEUCAMI *ALONE,* MASTER.

WHATEVER IS TRANSPIRING ON SALEUCAMI IS SOMETHING WE MUST KNOW *NOW.* EVEN A HANDFUL OF MORGUKAI TRAINED BY ANZATI ASSASSINS COULD BE DEVASTATING. BESIDES...

...WHO ELSE *IS* THERE?

CORUSCANT.
THE LOWER LEVELS.

THIS SECTOR WAS A LOT LIVELIER BEFORE THE "SECURITY ACTS" WERE PASSED. YOU COULD FIND ALMOST ANYTHING YOU WANTED DOWN HERE.

IT'S STILL TRUE, BUT NOW YOU NEED TO KNOW WHERE TO LOOK.

UNLESS IT FINDS YOU FIRST.

I AM SALJÉ TASHA. I UNDERSTAND YOU WANTED TO MEET WITH ME.

HEARD YOU COMING WAY OFF. I THOUGHT *ANZATI* WERE SNEAKIER THAN THAT.

NEVER MIND. I NEED AN *ASSASSIN,* AND YOU COME HIGHLY RECOMMENDED. CARE TO TALK TARGET AND TERMS?

UNNECESSARY. I *ALWAYS* RESEARCH A CONTACT *BEFORE* I MEET THEM. I KNOW THAT YOU TRAVEL WITH KORTO VOS -- FORGIVE ME, *QUINLAN* VOS, JEDI. *HE* WANTS THIS MEETING, KHALEEN HENTZ.

WHERE *IS* HE?

HERE.

IMPRESSIVE!

SO, *YOU* ARE VOS --

-- THE SLAYER OF THE LEGENDARY ANZATI JEDI VOLFE KARKKO.

BUT JEDI DO *NOT* HIRE ASSASSINS. SO *WHY* DO YOU SEEK ME?

I WANT THE *NAME* OF THE PERSON WHO HIRED YOU TO KILL CHANCELLOR VALORUM.

THE ANZATI *CODE OF HONOR* FORBIDS MY DISCUSSING A CONTRACT OR EVEN ACKNOWLEDGING A KILL.

I DON'T *CARE* WHAT YOUR CODES ARE. GIVE ME THE INFORMATION, OR I WILL *RIP* IT FROM YOU.

"AAYLA. YOU'RE THE ONLY JEDI CLOSE ENOUGH TO RECEIVE HIS TRANSMISSION. THE COUNCIL ... THE REPUBLIC ... NEEDS TO KNOW WHAT I'VE LEARNED HERE ON SALEUCAMI.

"THE SITUATION IS FAR WORSE THAN WE THOUGHT. SORA BULQ HAS AN INSTALLATION IN THE MAGMA CHAMBERS THAT HONEYCOMB THE SURFACE BENEATH THE CAPITAL CITY.

"THE MORGUKAI YOU FOUGHT ON ANZAT WAS A CLONE. THE SEPARATISTS ARE GROWING AN ARMY OF THEM ON SALEUCAMI.

"THE ANZATI ARE TEACHING THE MORGUKAI STEALTH AND ASSASSINATION TECHNIQUES -- ALL EQUIPPED WITH CORTOSIS-ALLOY BLADES.

"YOUR OLD OPPONENT BOK IS HERE -- NO DOUBT THE SOURCE OF THE CLONING MATERIAL. I LISTENED IN WHILE HE AND RATH KELKKO REPORTED TO SORA.

"DOOKU WAS PRESENT VIA HOLOCOMM."

YOUR MORGUKAI ADAPT QUICKLY TO OUR METHODS. MASTERY, OF COURSE, TAKES YEARS.

BUT THEY SHOULD BE COMPETENT IN THE ESSENTIALS SOON ENOUGH.

CORUSCANT.

I THOUGHT SORA BULQ WAS WORKING **FOR** DOOKU --

-- AND DIDN'T DOOKU GO TO THE DARK SIDE **FIRST**? DOES THIS MAKE **SENSE**, QUIN?

THE SITH ARE DEVIOUS. THEY LEAD US ON UNTIL WE BELIEVE IN LIES. I HAVE TO TRUST MY SENSES.

SORA BULQ **IS** THE OTHER SITH. HE MOVED WITHIN THE TEMPLE AS ONE OF US, UNTIL HE FOUND IN **DOOKU** A JEDI HE COULD TURN TO THE DARK SIDE.

FINDING HIM WON'T BE EASY. EVEN [WH]EN HE WAS WITH DOOKU, [SO]RA WAS HARD TO FIND. [I] HAVEN'T TURNED UP ANY [TR]ACE OF HIM IN THE PAST SIX MONTHS.

VOS.

MASTER VOS? MASTER OPPO RANCISIS HAS BEEN ASKING FOR YOU.

I'M ON MY WAY. VOS OUT.

Breep

COMMLINK. SOMEBODY FROM THE TEMPLE'S LOOKING FOR ME.

STAY WITH THE SKORP-ION, KHALEEN. KEEP EVERYTHING READY FOR TAKE-OFF.

I'LL SEE WHAT MASTER RANCISIS WANTS. IF NEED BE, WE'LL JUST TAKE OFF AND USE OUR OWN RESOURCES TO TRACK DOWN SORA BULQ.

THE TRANSMISSION ENDED THERE. NOTHING HAS BEEN HEARD FROM MASTER THOLME SINCE.

I FELT SOMETHING... FAINTLY... IN THE FORCE, I SHOULD HAVE KNOWN IT WAS YOU, THOLME.

I KNOW MY FORMER MASTER WELL. I'M WILLING TO BET HE'S STILL ALIVE AND CAUSING THEM GRIEF. IT'S HIS WAY.

I COULD LEAVE FOR SALEUCAMI ALMOST IMMEDIATELY, MAKE CONTACT WITH HIM --

YOU WILL -- ALONG WITH THREE BATTALIONS. THE SUPREME CHANCELLOR DEEMS THESE ANZATI-TRAINED MORGUKAI A MAJOR THREAT --

-- AND THE COUNCIL AGREES THEY MUST BE STOPPED, AND SORA BULQ DEALT WITH.

I WILL BE IN OVERALL COMMAND OF THE REPUBLIC FORCES. I WANT YOU AS MY SECOND IN COMMAND, MASTER VOS. YOUR KNOWLEDGE OF BOTH MORGUKAI AND ANZATI WILL BE INVALUABLE.

WE LEAVE IMMEDIATELY. ARE YOU WILLING?

AS YOU WISH, MASTER RANCISIS. I AM AT YOUR COMMAND.

DEEP WITHIN A HIDDEN LAIR ON CORUSCANT...

I AM PLEASED. VOS, WHETHER HE ACCEPTS IT OR NOT, IS OUR TOOL. HIS OBSESSION WILL MAKE HIM MALLEABLE. HE WILL FALL TO THE *DARK SIDE*.

GENERAL GRIEVOUS REPORTS ALL IS IN READINESS, MASTER. THE JEDI AND THE REPUBLIC WILL BECOME ENMESHED IN SIEGES ON THE OUTER RIM.

ONCE COMMITTED, THEY WILL FIND THEMSELVES UNABL' TO BREAK OFF. IT WILL LEAVE THEM VULNERABLE TO GRIEVOUS' STRIKE FORCE.

ALL THE PLAYERS ARE NOW IN PLACE. IT IS TIME TO INITIATE THE END MOVES. THE PLAN OF MANY LONG YEARS WILL BEAR FRUIT AT LAST!

THE TRIUMPH OF THE SITH WILL BE COMPLETE -- AND WE SHALL HAVE OUR *REVENGE!*

NEXT: THE SIEGE OF SALEUCAM

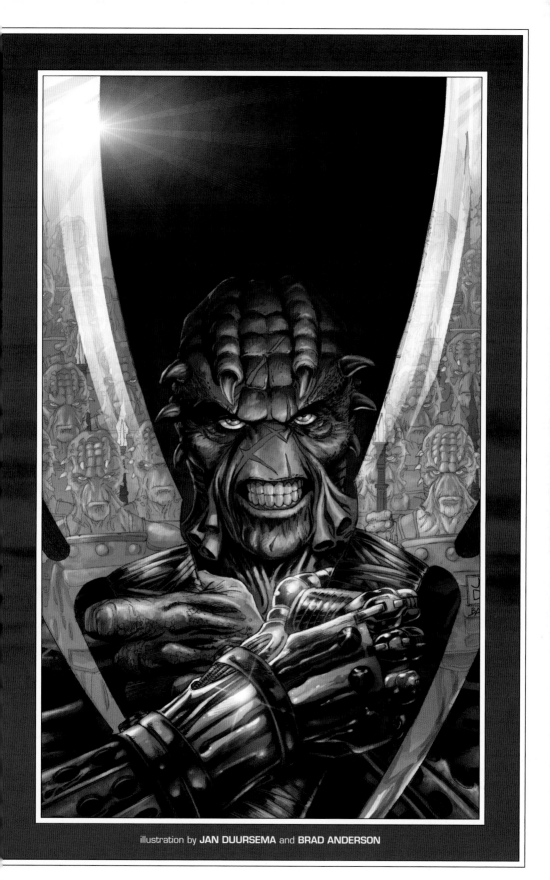

illustration by **JAN DUURSEMA** and **BRAD ANDERSON**

SIEGE OF SALEUCAMI

APPROXIMATELY THREE WEEKS
BEFORE THE EVENTS IN
REVENGE OF THE SITH . . .

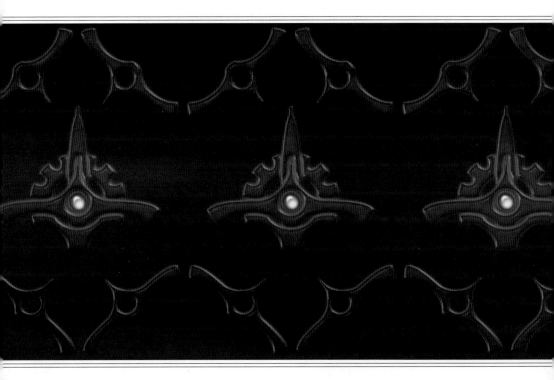

script by **John Ostrander**
pencils by **Jan Duursema**
inks by **Dan Parsons**

"FOR FIVE MONTHS, WE'VE LAID SIEGE TO SALEUCAMI.

"WE JEDI HAVE LED THE REPUBLIC'S CLONE ARMY AGAINST A MORGUKAI CLONE ARMY CREATED BY THE C.I.S. AND TRAINED BY ANZATI.

"THE SIEGE HAS PREVENTED THE SEPARATIST FORCES FROM LEAVING SALEUCAMI, BUT THE COST IN LIVES HAS BEEN HIGH, AND SUPPLIES ARE THIN. OUTSIDE OF THE CALDERA AND THE CITY IN IT, EVERYTHING'S SAND.

"AT DAWN TODAY, WE'LL ENGAGE THE ENEMY ONCE MORE. I **SUSPECT** WE'LL TRY **AGAIN** TO TAKE THE PERIMETER SHIELD GENERATOR AND ION GUNS THAT GUARD THE RIM OF THE CALDERA.

"GENERAL OPPO RANCISIS HAS SAID THAT A **PATH** BELOW WILL BE **REVEALED.** I DON'T KNOW. I CAN'T SEE IT -- CAN'T **FEEL** IT -- MYSELF. IT'S ALL JUST CHAOS. BUT HE SAYS WE **WILL** KNOW VICTORY.

"IF THE FORCE WILLS."
   -- GENERAL QUINLAN VOS
   SIEGE OF SALEUCAMI

EVEN IF WE COULD GET CLOSE ENOU TO FIRE ON TH ION CANNON, TH SHIELDS GO UP FAST WE'D BE TOASTED.

JEISEL, THIS IS *AAYLA*. WE HAVE TROUBLE UP HERE, AS WELL. ONLY ABOUT *HALF* OF THE SHIPS ARE MAKING IT PLANETSIDE. *AND* THEY'VE TAKEN DAMAGE.

IF YOUR GROUND TROOPS CAN KNOCK THE SHIELD DOWN, WE CAN BLAST THAT ION CANNON AND TAKE THE CALDERA RIM!

THAT'S WHY WE NEED THE RE-ENFORCEMENTS! TO TAKE DOWN THE SHIELD GENERATOR!

AUSAR AUSET!

HE IS ONE WITH THE FORCE, MASTER HETT.

"A PATH BELOW WILL BE REVEALED." JUST AS MASTER RANCISIS SAID...

THE BLAST EXPOSED ACCESS TUNNELS THE SEPS HAVE BEEN USING.

ACCORDING TO MY AGENTS, THE TUNNELS SHOULD GIVE US A WAY TO GET *UNDERNEATH* THE SHIELD AND BLOW THE GENERATOR.

JEISEL, YOU'RE WITH ME.

HETT AND K'KRUHK -- KEEP MORGUKAI OFF OUR BACKS.

WHAT ARE YOU DOING, KHALEEN?

OH, HI, QUIN!

JUST TRYING TO SEE IF I CAN MAKE THIS TOY WORK.

IT'S NOT A *TOY*, KHALEEN. IT'S CALLED A *HOLOCRON* --

-- ONLY JEDI CAN ACTIVATE IT.

MASTER RANCISIS FELT IT WOULD BE *USEFUL* IN HELPING ME "SORT OUT" ... THINGS.

MEANT TO BE A TEACHING DEVICE. JEDI RECORD THEIR EXPERIENCES INTO THEM. THEY'RE INTERACTIVE SO YOU CAN TALK WITH THEM.

DARKNESS SURROUNDS ME. NATURE'S VIOLENCE CHURNS ALL AROUND, ECHOING THE VIOLENCE ON THE SURFACE WORLD ABOVE.

OUTSIDE THESE CAVERNS, THE FORCE IS ... CLOUDED. DOWN HERE, I HAVE TAPPED INTO A FRIGHTENING CLARITY.

ON THE SURFACE, I SENSE THE SCREAMS OF BATTLE AND THE MOANS OF THE DYING. I FEEL DEATH WASHING OVER ME LIKE A DARK RIVER.

I FEEL OPPO RANCISIS, DEEP IN HIS BATTLE MEDITATION, BURNING BRIGHTLY IN THE FORCE. I SENSE THE DEPTH OF HIS THOUGHTS AND THE BREADTH OF HIS VISION.

I SENSE MY PADAWANS. AAYLA SECURA SHIMMERING IN THE FORCE -- A BEACON OF BLUE LIGHT.

HER TROOPS STARE DEATH IN THE FACE FOR HER AND FOLLOW HER INTO THE ABYSS. IT IS NOT SIMPLY HOW THEY WERE BRED; IT IS HOW THEY ARE LED. THEY FOLLOW NOT ONLY HER COMMANDS, BUT HER EXAMPLE.

AND THEN I FEEL HIM, BURNING ACROSS THE FIELD OF BATTLE, RAGING AND ANGRY IN THE FORCE.

QUINLAN VOS, MY FIRST PADAWAN.

I TAUGHT HIM TO BE A JEDI. I TAUGHT HIM TO CARRY THE LIGHT WITHIN HIM. I ALSO TAUGHT HIM HOW TO WALK IN THE SHADOWS. NOW I CAN ONLY SENSE CHURNING DARKNESS WITHIN HIM.

AH, QUINLAN -- WHAT HAVE YOU BECOME?

UGHN!

AAAAH!

UFF!

THIS WAY.

THE COUNT IS WAITING.

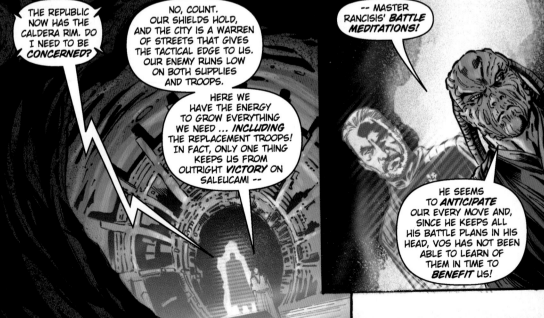

THE REPUBLIC NOW HAS THE CALDERA RIM. DO I NEED TO BE CONCERNED?

NO, COUNT. OUR SHIELDS HOLD, AND THE CITY IS A WARREN OF STREETS THAT GIVES THE TACTICAL EDGE TO US. OUR ENEMY RUNS LOW ON BOTH SUPPLIES AND TROOPS.

HERE WE HAVE THE ENERGY TO GROW EVERYTHING WE NEED ... INCLUDING THE REPLACEMENT TROOPS! IN FACT, ONLY ONE THING KEEPS US FROM OUTRIGHT VICTORY ON SALEUCAMI --

-- MASTER RANCISIS' BATTLE MEDITATIONS!

HE SEEMS TO ANTICIPATE OUR EVERY MOVE AND, SINCE HE KEEPS ALL HIS BATTLE PLANS IN HIS HEAD, VOS HAS NOT BEEN ABLE TO LEARN OF THEM IN TIME TO BENEFIT US!

I'VE BEEN DREADING THIS AND I DON'T KNOW WHY.

NOW YOU KNOW WHY THE FORCE HAS *LED* YOU TO THIS PLACE AND THIS TIME.

LOOK IN YOUR PADAWAN'S *EYES*, YOU MUST. KNOW, YOU WILL, IF TO THE DARK SIDE HE HAS FALLEN. *FEAR*, DO YOU, WHAT YOU WILL SEE.

QUINLAN.

MASTER.

NOW...
THERE IS ONLY
YOU AND I.

I WILL
ACCEPT YOUR
SURRENDER. OR
I WILL TAKE YOUR
LIFE. WHICH DO YOU
PREFER?

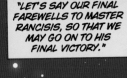

"LET'S SAY OUR FINAL FAREWELLS TO MASTER RANCISIS, SO THAT WE MAY GO ON TO HIS FINAL VICTORY."

THE FLAMES TAKE HOLD OF WHAT ONCE WAS OUR FRIEND, OUR BROTHER, OUR MASTER -- OPPO RANCISIS. IT TRANSMUTES THE BODY INTO ENERGY, AND ENERGY IS PART OF THE FORCE -- AS ARE WE ALL.

WITH HIM, WE REMEMBER THOSE OTHERS OF OUR ORDER WHO HAVE FALLEN HERE ON SALEUCAMI AND NAME THEM.

I REMEMBER ALISAR ALISET.

I REMEMBER XELTEK.

DURNAR.

THOLME.

T'BOLTON.

BRAVE **WORDS,** QUINLAN VOS. BUT WORDS DO NOT DECIDE THE ISSUE. YOU SAY YOU HAVE MADE YOUR CHOICE -- BUT CAN YOU MAKE YOUR CHOICE STICK?

I CAN STILL FEEL YOUR **ANGER** -- AND GOOD JEDI DO NOT FEEL ANGER, DO THEY? AS YOU SAY, NO MORE PRETENDING. YOU CROSSED OVER TO THE DARK SIDE LONG AGO. YOU JUST WON'T **ADMIT** IT.

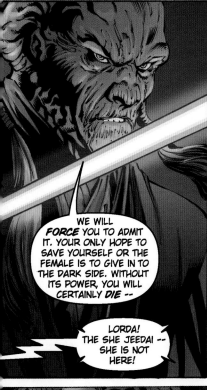

WE WILL **FORCE** YOU TO ADMIT IT. YOUR ONLY HOPE TO SAVE YOURSELF OR THE FEMALE IS TO GIVE IN TO THE DARK SIDE. WITHOUT ITS POWER, YOU WILL CERTAINLY **DIE** --

LORDA! THE SHE JEEDAI -- SHE IS NOT HERE!

I GO TO WHERE THE VOS SAY JEEDAI SECURA PLANT EXPLOSIVES --

-- BUT NO EXPLOSIVES! NO JEEDAI!

QUINLAN LIED.

THERE *IS* A SECOND SITH!

IT *IS* SORA BULQ! I RIPPED THE TRUTH FROM SAJÈ TASHA'S MIND!

IT WAS *LEFT* THERE FOR YOU TO FIND! THE COUNT *KNEW* OF YOUR OBSESSION --

-- AND THAT YOU WOULD BETRAY EVERYTHING AND EVERYONE TO SATISFY IT!

I BETRAYED *NO ONE!* I USED *HIM!*

DID YOU? AT YOUR CORE YOU ARE ONE OF *US,* VOS!

YOU SAY YOU HAVE DISAVOWED THE DARK SIDE, VOS --

-- BUT IT IS THE *TRUTH* YOU DESPERATELY *DENY* ... EVEN NOW!

SHUT UP!

DO AS YOUR TRUE **MASTER** COMMANDS, VOS! DRAW UPON THE DARK SIDE!

OR I WILL KILL YOU -- AND ALL THOSE YOU SEEK TO DEFEND!

HRAI!

I TAKE NO JOY IN THIS, BOK. ACCORDING TO LEGEND, THERE WAS ALWAYS **SOME** HONOR IN THE MORGUKAI. WHY DO YOU SERVE SO DISHONORABLE A MASTER?

BOK WAS PROMISED MORGUKAI BE **RESURRECTED!** BUT MORGUKAI CLONES NOT TRUE MORGUKAI.

NOW THERE IS ONLY **REVENGE.** ALL ELSE DEAD.

YOU **KNEW** OF THE DARKNESS WITHIN VOS, AND YOU ENCOURAGED HIM TO GO **DEEPER** WITHIN IT. YOU **USED** HIM AS A WEAPON AGAINST ME.

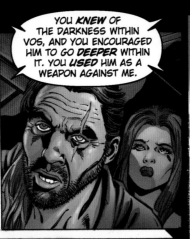

DO YOU UNDERSTAND ME, QUINLAN? YOU WERE BETRAYED BY YOUR OWN MASTER FROM THE START!

AND HE SHOULD **TRUST** YOU, THOLME?

NO GOOD!

MY LIGHTSABER STILL WON'T IGNITE! I CAN'T REACH YOU, QUIN -- NOT **PHYSICALLY**.

BUT THERE ARE THE THINGS THAT BIND US -- MIND AND HEART -- MASTER AND PADAWAN! MUST CLEAR MY MIND AS MASTER RANCISIS DID... REACH OUT WITH MY FEELINGS AS MASTER YODA TAUGHT... AS MASTER THOLME TAUGHT...!

AS YOU TAUGHT

AAYLA?

VERY GOOD. YES ... I UNDERSTAND... LET ME JOIN WITH YOU!

JOIN WHO? WHERE DO YOU THINK YOU'RE GOING, OLD MAN?

OH NO! NO NO NO! DON'T YOU **DIE** ON ME, OLD MAN! DON'T YOU **DARE**! YOU HEAR ME?! WE **NEED** YOU! **THOLME**!

I WANT TO THANK YOU, AAYLA. YOU *AND* THOLME. IF NOT FOR YOU...

IT WAS *YOUR* CHOICE, QUIN! WE JUST REMINDED YOU OF WHO AND WHAT YOU *TRULY* ARE.

AAYLA IS CORRECT, QUINLAN. WE THREE SHARE A BOND IN THE FORCE. THROUGH THIS LINK WE WILL ALWAYS FEEL ONE ANOTHER IN OUR HEARTS.

IT IS STILL THERE, MASTER. THE DARKNESS WITHIN ME. I'D HOPED I KILLED IT BUT...

THE TRUTH IS THAT THE LURE OF THE DARK SIDE WILL ALWAYS BE THERE FOR YOU.

IT IS PART OF YOUR NATURE AND ALWAYS WILL BE. YOU WILL BATTLE IT MOMENT BY MOMENT ALL YOUR LIFE.

I KNOW. IT'S ONE OF THE REASONS I'VE DECIDED THAT --

-- WHEN THIS WAR IS OVER, I AM GOING TO LEAVE THE JEDI ORDER.

ARE YOU CERTAIN --?!

YES. VERY CERTAIN. THERE'S ANOTHER REASON. WHEN I LOOKED INTO KHALEEN'S HEART, I SAW SOMETHING ELSE -- A SECRET *SHE* WAS HIDING.

SHE CARRIES OUR CHILD.

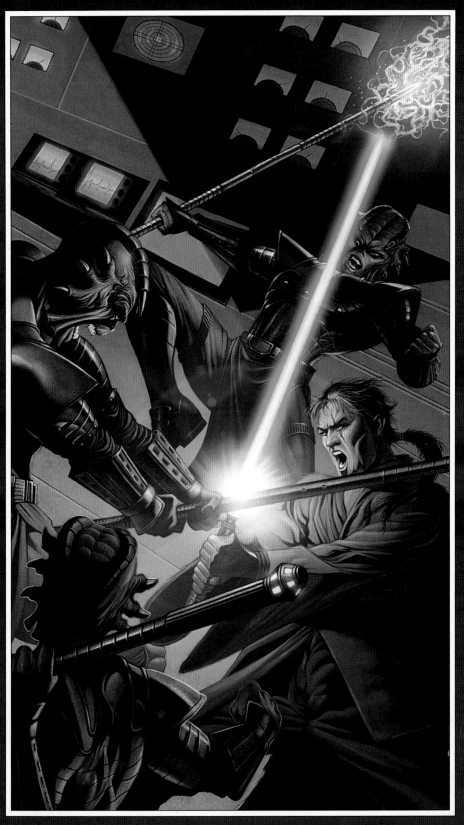

illustration by **DAVID MICHAEL BECK** and **BRAD ANDERSON**

illustration by **JAN DUURSEMA** and **BRAD ANDERSON**

STAR WARS®

D REPUBLIC ERA:
000—1000 YEARS BEFORE
AR WARS: A NEW HOPE

es of the Jedi—
e Golden Age of the Sith
N: 1-56971-229-8 $16.95

es of the Jedi—
e Fall of the Sith Empire
N: 1-56971-320-0 $14.95

es of the Jedi—
ghts of the Old Republic
N: 1-56971-020-1 $14.95

es of the Jedi—
e Freedon Nadd Uprising
N: 1-56971-307-3 $5.95

es of the Jedi—
rk Lords of the Sith
N: 1-56971-095-3 $17.95

es of the Jedi—The Sith War
N: 1-56971-173-9 $17.95

es of the Jedi—Redemption
N: 1-56971-535-1 $14.95

i vs. Sith
N: 1-56971-649-8 $17.95

E OF THE EMPIRE ERA:
00-0 YEARS BEFORE
AR WARS: A NEW HOPE

e Stark Hyperspace War
N: 1-56971-985-3 $12.95

i Council—Acts of War
N: 1-56971-539-4 $12.95

lude to Rebellion
N: 1-56971-448-7 $14.95

rth Maul
N: 1-56971-542-4 $12.95

sode I—The Phantom Menace
N: 1-56971-359-6 $12.95

sode I—
e Phantom Menace Adventures
N: 1-56971-443-6 $12.95

go Fett
N: 1-56971-623-4 $5.95

n Wesell
N: 1-56971-624-2 $5.95

Jango Fett—Open Seasons
ISBN: 1-56971-671-4 $12.95

Outlander
ISBN: 1-56971-514-9 $14.95

Emissaries to Malastare
ISBN: 1-56971-545-9 $15.95

The Bounty Hunters
ISBN: 1-56971-467-3 $12.95

Twilight
ISBN: 1-56971-558-0 $12.95

The Hunt for Aurra Sing
ISBN: 1-56971-651-X $12.95

Darkness
ISBN: 1-56971-659-5 $12.95

Rite of Passage
ISBN: 1-59307-042-X $12.95

Honor and Duty
ISBN: 1-59307-546-4 $12.95

Episode II—Attack of the Clones
ISBN: 1-56971-609-9 $17.95

Clone Wars Volume 1—
The Defense of Kamino
ISBN: 1-56971-962-4 $14.95

Clone Wars Volume 2—
Victories and Sacrifices
ISBN: 1-56971-969-1 $14.95

Clone Wars Volume 3—
Last Stand on Jabiim
ISBN: 1-59307-006-3 $14.95

Clone Wars Volume 4—Light and Dark
ISBN: 1-59307-195-7 $16.95

Clone Wars Volume 5—The Best Blades
ISBN: 1-59307-273-2 $17.95

Clone Wars Volume 6—
On the Fields of Battle
ISBN: 1-59307-352-6 $17.95

Clone Wars Volume 7—
When They Were Brothers
ISBN: 1-59307-396-8 $17.95

Clone Wars Volume 8—
The Last Siege, The Final Truth
ISBN: 1-59307-482-4 $17.95

Clone Wars Volume 9—Endgame
ISBN: 1-59307-553-7 $17.95

Clone Wars Adventures Volume 1
ISBN: 1-59307-243-0 $6.95

Clone Wars Adventures Volume 2
ISBN: 1-59307-271-6 $6.95

Clone Wars Adventures Volume 3
ISBN: 1-59307-307-0 $6.95

Clone Wars Adventures Volume 4
ISBN: 1-59307-402-6 $6.95

Clone Wars Adventures Volume 5
ISBN: 1-59307-483-2 $6.95

Clone Wars Adventures Volume 6
ISBN: 1-59307-567-7 $6.95

Episode III—Revenge of the Sith
ISBN: 1-59307-309-7 $12.95

General Grievous
ISBN: 1-59307-442-5 $12.95

Droids—The Kalarba Adventures
ISBN: 1-56971-064-3 $17.95

Droids—Rebellion
ISBN: 1-56971-224-7 $14.95

Classic Star Wars—
Han Solo at Stars' End
ISBN: 1-56971-254-9 $6.95

Boba Fett—Enemy of the Empire
ISBN: 1-56971-407-X $12.95

Underworld—The Yavin Vassilika
ISBN: 1-56971-618-8 $15.95

Dark Forces—Soldier for the Empire
ISBN: 1-56971-348-0 $14.95

Empire Volume 1—Betrayal
ISBN: 1-56971-964-0 $12.95

Empire Volume 2—Darklighter
ISBN: 1-56971-975-6 $17.95

REBELLION ERA:
0-5 YEARS AFTER
STAR WARS: A NEW HOPE

A New Hope—The Special Edition
ISBN: 1-56971-213-1 $9.95

Empire Volume 3—
The Imperial Perspective
ISBN: 1-59307-128-0 $17.95

Empire Volume 4—
The Heart of the Rebellion
ISBN: 1-59307-308-9 $17.95

Empire Volume 5—Allies and Adversaries
ISBN: 1-59307-466-2 $14.95

A Long Time Ago... Volume 1—
Doomworld
ISBN: 1-56971-754-0 $29.95

A Long Time Ago... Volume 2—
Dark Encounters
ISBN: 1-56971-785-0 $29.95

Classic Star Wars—
The Early Adventures
ISBN: 1-56971-178-X $19.95

Classic Star Wars Volume 1—
In Deadly Pursuit
ISBN: 1-56971-109-7 $16.95

Classic Star Wars Volume 2—
The Rebel Storm
ISBN: 1-56971-106-2 $16.95

Classic Star Wars Volume 3—
Escape to Hoth
ISBN: 1-56971-093-7 $16.95

Jabba the Hutt—The Art of the Deal
ISBN: 1-56971-310-3 $9.95

Vader's Quest
ISBN: 1-56971-415-0 $11.95

Splinter of the Mind's Eye
ISBN: 1-56971-223-9 $14.95

The Empire Strikes Back—
The Special Edition
ISBN: 1-56971-234-4 $9.95

A Long Time Ago... Volume 3—
Resurrection of Evil
ISBN: 1-56971-786-9 $29.95

A Long Time Ago... Volume 4—
Screams in the Void
ISBN: 1-56971-787-7 $29.95

A Long Time Ago... Volume 5—
Fool's Bounty
ISBN: 1-56971-906-3 $29.95

Battle of the Bounty Hunters
Pop-Up Book
ISBN: 1-56971-129-1 $17.95

Shadows of the Empire
ISBN: 1-56971-183-6 $17.95

Return of the Jedi—The Special Edition
ISBN: 1-56971-235-2 $9.95

A Long Time Ago... Volume 6—
Wookiee World
ISBN: 1-56971-907-1 $29.95

A Long Time Ago... Volume 7—
Far, Far Away
ISBN: 1-56971-908-X $29.95

Mara Jade—By the Emperor's Hand
ISBN: 1-56971-401-0 $15.95

Shadows of the Empire: Evolution
ISBN: 1-56971-441-X $14.95

NEW REPUBLIC ERA:
5-25 YEARS AFTER
STAR WARS: A NEW HOPE

Omnibus—X-Wing Rogue Squadron
Volume 1
ISBN: 1-59307-572-3 $24.95

X-Wing Rogue Squadron—
Battleground Tatooine
ISBN: 1-56971-276-X $12.95

X-Wing Rogue Squadron—
The Warrior Princess
ISBN: 1-56971-330-8 $12.95

X-Wing Rogue Squadron—
Requiem for a Rogue
ISBN: 1-56971-331-6 $12.95

X-Wing Rogue Squadron—
In the Empire's Service
ISBN: 1-56971-383-9 $12.95

X-Wing Rogue Squadron—
Blood and Honor
ISBN: 1-56971-387-1 $12.95

X-Wing Rogue Squadron—
Masquerade
ISBN: 1-56971-487-8 $12.95

X-Wing Rogue Squadron—
Mandatory Retirement
ISBN: 1-56971-492-4 $12.95

Dark Forces—Rebel Agent
ISBN: 1-56971-400-2 $14.95

Dark Forces—Jedi Knight
ISBN: 1-56971-433-9 $14.95

Heir to the Empire
ISBN: 1-56971-202-6 $19.95

Dark Force Rising
ISBN: 1-56971-269-7 $17.95

The Last Command
ISBN: 1-56971-378-2 $17.95

Boba Fett—
Death, Lies, and Treachery
ISBN: 1-56971-311-1 $12.95

Dark Empire
ISBN: 1-59307-039-X $16.95

Dark Empire II
ISBN: 1-59307-526-X $19.95

Empire's End
ISBN: 1-56971-306-5 $5.95

Crimson Empire
ISBN: 1-56971-355-3 $17.95

Crimson Empire II: Council of Blood
ISBN: 1-56971-410-X $17.95

Jedi Academy: Leviathan
ISBN: 1-56971-456-8 $11.95

Union
ISBN: 1-56971-464-9 $12.95

NEW JEDI ORDER ERA:
25+ YEARS AFTER
STAR WARS: A NEW HOPE

Chewbacca
ISBN: 1-56971-515-7 $12.95

INFINITIES:
DOES NOT APPLY TO TIMELINE

Infinites: A New Hope
ISBN: 1-56971-648-X $12.95

Infinities: The Empire Strikes Back
ISBN: 1-56971-904-7 $12.95

Infinities: Return of the Jedi
ISBN: 1-59307-206-6 $12.95

Star Wars Tales Volume 1
ISBN: 1-56971-619-6 $19.95

Star Wars Tales Volume 2
ISBN: 1-56971-757-5 $19.95

Star Wars Tales Volume 3
ISBN: 1-56971-836-9 $19.95

Star Wars Tales Volume 4
ISBN: 1-56971-989-6 $19.95

Star Wars Tales Volume 5
ISBN: 1-59307-286-4 $19.95

Star Wars Tales Volume 6
ISBN: 1-59307-447-6 $19.95

FOR MORE INFORMATION ABOUT THESE BOOKS VISIT DARKHORSE.COM!